Small & Scrappy

Pint-Size Patchwork Quilts
Using Reproduction Fabrics

Kathleen Tracy

Martingale
Create with Confidence

DEDICATION

To my mom, for encouraging my creativity and especially for always giving in and buying me the biggest box of Crayola crayons every September, which instilled in me a love of playing with color at an early age.

Small and Scrappy:
Pint-Size Patchwork Quilts Using Reproduction Fabrics
© 2016 by Kathleen Tracy

Martingale®
19021 120th Ave. NE, Ste. 102
Bothell, WA 98011-9511 USA
ShopMartingale.com

Printed in China
21 20 19 18 17 16   8 7 6 5 4 3 2 1

Library of Congress Cataloging-in-Publication Data is available upon request.

ISBN: 978-1-60468-825-2

MISSION STATEMENT

We empower makers who use fabric and yarn to make life more enjoyable.

CREDITS

PUBLISHER AND
CHIEF VISIONARY OFFICER
Jennifer Erbe Keltner

CONTENT DIRECTOR
Karen Costello Soltys

DESIGN MANAGER
Adrienne Smitke

MANAGING EDITOR
Tina Cook

COVER AND
INTERIOR DESIGNER
Regina Girard

ACQUISITIONS EDITOR
Karen M. Burns

PHOTOGRAPHER
Brent Kane

TECHNICAL EDITOR
Nancy Mahoney

ILLUSTRATOR
Lisa Lauch

COPY EDITOR
Durby Peterson

SPECIAL THANKS

Thanks to Mara Lee Gibson, owner of The Country Cupboard/Cin-a-mon Stik in Snohomish, Washington, and Melanie Bryan, owner of M&M Antiques in Monroe, Washington, for graciously allowing Martingale to take photographs for this book in their respective stores. You can follow both The Country Cupboard and M&M Antiques on Facebook.

Contents

Introduction

Antique quilts from the past have inspired quilters for years. More often than not, antique quilts were scrap quilts, and these are the quilts so many quilters love today. Before we knew much about quilting history, it was a common belief that most antique quilts were made from quilters' overflowing baskets of scraps cut from old, worn clothing. While that's a lovely, romantic notion about the past, it's more likely that many of these quilts were very well planned out and that the fabric used was often new, bought with certain projects in mind.

By the middle of the nineteenth century, the amount of fabric available rapidly increased, and the women who could afford to acquire a variety of fabric had the freedom to make creative decisions about what went into their quilts. Most quilts were designed deliberately and probably not sewn together as haphazardly as we've come to believe. Upon inspection, many antique quilts show clear evidence of brilliant design capability and conscious choice in fabric selection. Did the women who made these quilts play with their fabric? Judging from the quilts, it appears they did just that.

Scrap quilting is truly an American tradition. During the latter part of the nineteenth century, particularly after the Civil War, fabric was scarce or costly. Not all quilters were wealthy enough to afford new fabric for every quilt that needed to be made. The most abundant quilts we see from this period were the utilitarian scrap quilts made by the average woman.

Families typically gathered their remnants of fabric from cast-off clothing or other sewing projects and stored them in a bag of scraps or scrap basket. Fabric from Mama's or Aunt Betsy's dresses or even Papa's shirts sometimes made their way into the quilts. Quilts often became records of family histories, with their squares and triangles cut from pieces of dresses or other clothing. What a comfort it must have been to sleep under warm bedding that contained memories of loved ones who were either gone or living far away.

Small quilts or doll quilts especially relied on these types of scraps because often that's all that was available after the larger projects were completed. Young girls learned to sew and perfected their stitches by making clothing or quilts for their dolls. Making simple doll quilts was a fun way to introduce children to the art of sewing, a necessary skill for all women and girls in early American households.

If you're new to quilting, or if any of the techniques are unfamiliar to you, I hope this book will encourage you to experience the joys of making small quilts. Remember, doll quilts don't need to be perfect to be charming. The joy of quilting is in the creating, and the satisfaction is in the learning. I had so much fun designing and making the projects for this book, and I know these simple quilts will inspire those of you who love working with small pieces and traditional patterns to recapture that old-fashioned look of the past.

Fabric Tips and Tricks

As quilters, we are collectors of fabric. Don't apologize for it or feel ashamed if you have "too much" fabric or "too many" scraps. Buying fabric is an essential part of the quilter's creative process, and it often gives us the inspiration we need to begin something new. Recognize that the size of your fabric collection isn't necessarily the problem—it may be that you simply need a better solution for storing it.

Organization Starts at the Fabric Store

For a long time, every fabric I loved I bought by the yard or more. I'd cut into the yardage and use a few pieces in my blocks. The rest of the fabric accumulated, and the smaller leftover pieces were stuffed into bins or baskets. When I needed a scrap for another, I had to dig through those crumpled pieces. It became apparent that when I threw my scraps into a large container and let them accumulate, I rarely used them. Digging through a 10-gallon bin of assorted scraps for just the right shade of green became counterproductive. It took too long, and I became overwhelmed and distracted by all the other colors. The scraps multiplied.

The solution? I started buying smaller cuts of fabric. Bundles, fat quarters, quarter yards, and even fat eighths or eighth-yard cuts allowed me to accumulate a substantial variety of different-colored fabrics, which is what I love to use in scrappy quilts. Usually, if I'm making a scrappy small quilt, all I need is a few inches of just the right red fabric, along with a couple of inches of another red print. If you make a lot of small quilts, purchasing smaller cuts of fabric allows you to buy a wider variety without too much expense. Smaller pieces of fabric are easier to store, and they make it easier to create scrappy quilts that don't all look the same.

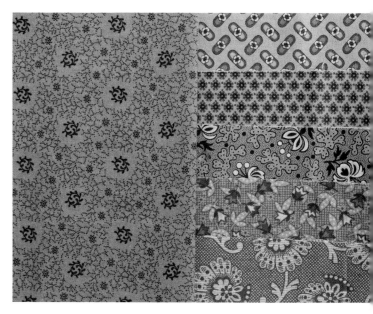

The blue fabric at left is pretty, but see how much livelier the mix of prints beside it appears? Build depth into your stash by collecting small pieces of many fabrics rather than large pieces of just a few.

Sorting and Storing

I've stopped throwing my scraps into a jumbled mess in a bin, having learned to treat them with the same respect I give new, unused fabric. When cutting fabric, I place leftovers in a small scrap basket. After I've finished a project, I go through the basket to sort and store the scraps. I find that it's a lot easier to organize a small basket of scraps on a regular basis than it is to go through a huge tub of scraps once a year.

Some quilters organize fabric according to the size of the strips or squares. Others, like myself, organize by color, designating a separate container for each hue. If you work with many different types of fabric, such as batiks, reproductions, and novelty prints, sorting solely by color may not be practical. A better solution might be to delegate a container or shelf to a particular type of fabric and then subdivide the different colors into drawers, bins, or bags. Whatever storage method you choose, make sure it is one that you will keep up and that makes your fabric easy to access.

I use a three-tiered system for storing fabric: wire baskets, clear bins, and transparent plastic bags. Fat quarters and larger cuts fit neatly in wire drawer units. Then, when I cut into a fat quarter and use more than half of it, I store what remains in a clear bin or other small drawer unit.

If most of a fabric gets used, I put the tiniest pieces that I can't bear to give up into a resealable plastic bag with other same-color scraps. These bags can all be stored in one bin.

If your organizing method isn't working for you, here are a few suggestions:

- Make a point of sorting your scraps or leftovers every time you finish a project.

- Get rid of unwanted fabric or unusable pieces. Just because your friend Claire gifted you with a bag of her leftovers doesn't mean you're obligated to use or keep all of them. Pick through and keep what you will use; then donate the rest to a school or charitable organization.

- If you make a lot of Log Cabin quilts, cut your scraps into strips before storing them. If much of your quilting time is spent making scrappy Nine Patch quilts, then cut your scraps into strips or squares according to the most common size you use. I trim scraps into different-sized squares because that makes it quick and easy to use them in making scrappy blocks.

Group small pieces by color and store them in plastic bags so it's easy to see what you have (left). Keep larger pieces in bins or baskets (right). Make it easy to start new projects by precutting scraps into strips and squares (bottom).

Building a Fabric Wardrobe

If you're like most quilters, you can easily get carried away when you shop, buying what you like but not necessarily what you'll need when you get home and start a project. So focus on building your fabric collection, especially if you're just starting out. How to do that? The next time you're in a quilt shop, buy several different prints of just one color. Then the next time you shop, buy several different prints of another color. If you continue to buy fabric this way, in time you'll establish a collection that, like a classic wardrobe, will take you anywhere.

Many quilters, myself included, tend to buy the same colors over and over. If you're intent on making scrap quilts, you'll need to branch out from your favorites and make sure your stash includes a complete range of colors and prints because it's easier to make scrappy quilts if you have a wide range of colors. Make sure you have a selection of different prints in the following: red, blue, green, pink, purple, rust (or orange), brown, tan, gold (or yellow), black, and a variety of light or shirting prints. These are all the colors in the color wheel. Select different types of prints for each color, such as geometrics, vines, or small florals. Include a few dots, stripes, and checks.

SCRAPPY PIN CUSHIONS

When creating a scrappy quilt, make more blocks than you need. Play around with them in different layouts until you find one that is pleasing. Then, after you've selected the blocks you want to use, don't discard the leftovers. They can easily be made into pincushions, smaller companion quilts, or even runners.

Flying Geese

FINISHED QUILT: 18" × 18½" ⚓ **FINISHED BLOCK: 1½" × 3"**

Patterns for traditional quilt blocks from the nineteenth century were often reflections of daily life, and some of the most popular blocks that were handed down from earlier times were named accordingly. Names such as Flying Geese, Birds in the Air, Broken Dishes, Churn Dash, and Log Cabin give us strong visual clues as to exactly what inspired these designs. Playing with and choosing colorful scraps for the "geese" gives this little quilt a playful look that lets your creativity soar.

Materials
Yardage is based on 42"-wide fabric.
⅓ yard *total* of assorted light prints for blocks
⅓ yard *total* of assorted medium or dark prints
    for blocks
⅛ yard of blue print for sashing
⅛ yard of multicolored plaid for border
¼ yard of yellow print for binding
⅔ yard of fabric for backing
21" × 22" piece of low-loft cotton batting

Cutting
From the assorted light prints, cut:
72 squares, 2" × 2" (36 sets of 2 matching squares)

From the assorted medium or dark prints, cut:
36 rectangles, 2" × 3½"

From the blue print, cut:
1 strip, 2¼" × 42"; cut into 2 pieces, 18½" long

From the plaid, cut:
1 strip, 3" × 42"; cut into 2 pieces, 18½" long

From the yellow print, cut:
3 strips, 1¼" × 42"

Making the Flying Geese Blocks
Draw a diagonal line from corner to corner on the wrong side of two matching light squares. Place one marked square on one end of a medium or dark rectangle, right sides together. Stitch on the marked line. Trim ¼" from the stitching line. Flip the triangle up and press the seam allowances toward the corner. Repeat on the opposite end of the rectangle, positioning the square as shown. Make 36 Flying Geese blocks.

Make 36.

Pieced and hand quilted by Kathleen Tracy

Assembling the Quilt Top

After sewing each seam, press the seam allowances as indicated by the arrows.

1. Lay out the Flying Geese blocks in three vertical rows of 12 blocks each. Sew the blocks together and press the seam allowances toward the long flat sides of the triangles rather than toward the pointed ends. The row should measure 3½" × 18½".

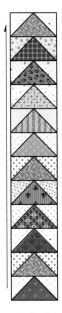

Make 3.

2. Sew the vertical rows and blue strips together as shown. The quilt should measure 13" × 18½".

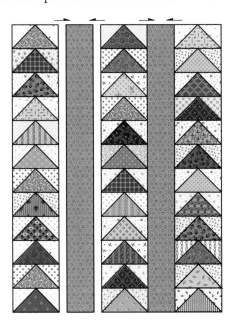

3. Sew the plaid strips to opposite sides of the quilt. The quilt top should be 18" × 18½".

Quilt assembly

Finishing the Quilt

1. For free, downloadable help with the following steps, go to ShopMartingale.com/HowtoQuilt. Layer the quilt top, batting and backing; baste the layers together.

2. Quilt a line through the center of each vertical row of blocks and in the ditch along the rows; outline the triangles. Mark 3" increments in the sashing and quilt an X in each space to make a diamond design. Quilt diagonal lines in the plaid borders, spacing the lines 1" apart.

3. Attach the binding to the quilt, referring to "Single-Fold Binding" on page 78.

Be My Little Valentine

FINISHED QUILT: 14½" × 15⅜" ❧ FINISHED BLOCK: 2" × 2"

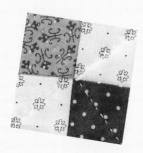

The Four Patch block is one of the most common blocks known to quilters. When pieced in a variety of ways with an assortment of different prints of the same color, even a simple quilt like this one can be made to shine.

Materials

Yardage is based on 42"-wide fabric.

¼ yard of light print for setting triangles and corner blocks

¼ yard of light pink print for border

⅛ yard *total* of assorted light prints for blocks

⅛ yard *total* of assorted pink prints for blocks

⅛ yard *total* of assorted red prints for blocks

⅜ yard of floral stripe for sashing*

⅛ yard of red print for binding

⅝ yard of fabric for backing

18" × 19" piece of low-loft cotton batting

Washable fabric marker

If you are using an allover print rather than a stripe, you'll only need ⅛ yard.

Cutting

From the assorted light prints, cut:
24 squares, 1½" × 1½"

From the assorted pink prints, cut:
13 squares, 1½" × 1½"

From the assorted red prints, cut:
11 squares, 1½" × 1½"

From the light print for setting triangles and corner blocks, cut:
5 squares, 4⅛" × 4⅛"; cut the squares into quarters diagonally to yield 20 side triangles (2 will be extra)
6 squares, 2⅜" × 2⅜"; cut the squares in half diagonally to yield 12 corner triangles
4 squares, 2¼" × 2¼"

From the floral stripe, cut *on the lengthwise grain:*
2 strips, 1⅝" × 11⅞"

From the light pink print, cut:
2 strips, 2¼" × 11⅞"
2 strips, 2¼" × 11¼"

From the red print, cut:
2 strips, 1¼" × 42"

Pieced and hand quilted by Kathleen Tracy

Making the Blocks

Join two light and two pink or red 1½" squares as shown to make a Four Patch block. Press the seam allowances as indicated by the arrows. Make 12 blocks. The blocks should measure 2" square.

Make 12.

Assembling the Quilt Top

After sewing each seam, press the seam allowances as indicated by the arrows.

1. Sew four blocks, six light 4⅛" side triangles, and four light 2⅜" corner triangles together in a vertical row as shown. Trim and square up the row, making sure to leave ¼" beyond the points of all the blocks for the seam allowances. Make three rows. The rows should measure approximately 3⅜" × 11⅞".

Make 3.

2. Sew the vertical rows and floral 1⅝"-wide strips together. The quilt should measure 11¼" × 11⅞".

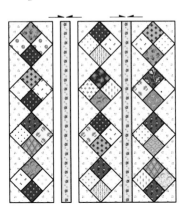

3. Sew light pink 2¼" × 11⅞" strips to opposite sides of the quilt. Sew a light 2¼" square to each end of a light pink 2¼" × 11¼" strip. Make two and sew them to the top and bottom of the quilt.

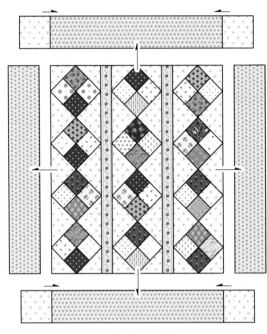

Quilt assembly

Finishing the Quilt

1. For free, downloadable help with the following steps, go to ShopMartingale.com/HowtoQuilt. Layer the quilt top, batting, and backing; baste the layers together.

2. Using cream hand-quilting thread, quilt in the ditch around the center of the quilt. Quilt an X in each block and along the inside of the vertical rows. Mark and then quilt a single wavy line along the floral print strips and a double wavy line in the borders. (I used a stencil to mark my lines.) With a washable fabric marker, draw a heart shape in the corner blocks. Using red thread, stitch on the drawn line to outline the hearts.

3. Attach the binding to the quilt, referring to "Single-Fold Binding" on page 78.

Scrappy Pinwheels

FINISHED QUILT: 20" × 26"   FINISHED BLOCK: 3" × 3"

Simple blocks are quick and fun to make. And, when you use a variety of different fabric scraps, an easy block like this Pinwheel pattern makes your quilt appear more complicated than it really is. Use contrast and color placement throughout your quilt to make the blocks look like they're spinning straight out of a nineteenth-century scrap basket.

Materials

Yardage is based on 42"-wide fabric.

⅜ yard *total* of assorted medium or dark prints for blocks

⅓ yard *total* of assorted light prints for blocks

¼ yard of tan print for border

¼ yard of red print for binding

⅛ yard *total* of assorted blue, tan, red, or green prints for blocks

6" × 6" square of blue print for corner blocks

¾ yard of fabric for backing

23" × 29" piece of low-loft cotton batting

Cutting

From the assorted light prints, cut:

60 squares, 2⅜" × 2⅜" (30 sets of 2 matching squares)

From the assorted blue, tan, red, or green prints, cut:

10 squares, 2⅜" × 2⅜" (5 sets of 2 matching squares)

From the assorted medium or dark prints, cut:

70 squares, 2⅜" × 2⅜" (35 sets of 2 matching squares)

From the tan print, cut:

2 strips, 2¾" × 42"; crosscut each strip into:

    1 strip, 2¾" × 21½" (2 total)

    1 strip, 2¾" × 15½" (2 total)

From the blue 6" square, cut:

4 squares, 2¾" × 2¾"

From the red print, cut:

3 strips, 1¼" × 42"

Making the Blocks

This is a fun and easy project that's ideal for using up some of your favorite reproduction-print scraps. To create contrast, I mixed several medium prints (blue, tan, red, and green) with the light prints for block backgrounds and placed them near the center of the quilt. For each Pinwheel block, I chose two matching light (or blue, tan, red, or green) 2⅜" squares paired with two matching medium or dark 2⅜" squares.

After sewing each seam, press the seam allowances as indicated by the arrows.

1. Draw a diagonal line from corner to corner on the wrong side of each light, blue, tan, red, and green 2⅜" square. Layer a marked square on top of a medium or dark 2⅜" square. Stitch ¼" from

Pieced and hand quilted by Kathleen Tracy

both sides of the line. Cut the squares apart on the drawn line. Trim the dog-ear pieces at the corners. Make four matching half-square-triangle units for each block (70 total). Units should be 2" square.

Make 4 for each block.

2. Sew four matching half-square-triangle units together as shown to make a Pinwheel block, which should measure 3½" square. Make 35 blocks.

Make 35.

Assembling the Quilt Top

After sewing each seam, press the seam allowances as indicated by the arrows.

1. Join five blocks to make a row that measures 15½" long. Make seven rows, pressing the seam allowances in opposite directions from row to row.

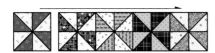

Make 7 rows.

2. Sew the rows together as shown, matching the seam intersections. The quilt should measure 15½" × 21½".

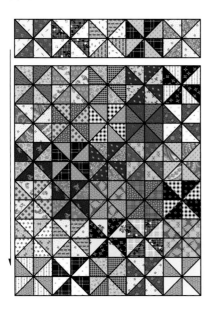

3. Sew tan 2¾" × 21½" strips to opposite sides of the quilt. Sew a blue 2¾" square to each end of a tan 2¾" × 15½" strip. Make two and sew them to the top and bottom of the quilt.

Quilt assembly

Finishing the Quilt

1. For free, downloadable help with the following steps, go to ShopMartingale.com/HowtoQuilt. Layer the quilt top, batting, and backing; baste the layers together.

2. Quilt diagonal lines 2" apart across the center of the quilt. Quilt parallel lines ½" apart lengthwise through the borders and an X in each of the corner blocks.

3. Attach the binding to the quilt, referring to "Single-Fold Binding" on page 78.

Blue and White

FINISHED QUILT: 13½" × 13½" ❧ FINISHED NINE PATCH BLOCKS: 3" × 3"

FINISHED RAIL FENCE BLOCKS: 3" × 4" ❧ FINISHED SAWTOOTH STAR BLOCK: 4" × 4"

Every quilter (or dolly!) needs a pretty blue-and-white quilt in her collection. This adorable little quilt was patterned after a doll quilt that had been cut from a block in a larger and well-worn antique cutter quilt.

Materials

Yardage is based on 42"-wide fabric.

⅓ yard of light print for blocks, borders, and binding

¼ yard of blue print for blocks

½ yard of fabric for backing

17" × 17" piece of low-loft cotton batting

Cutting

From the blue print, cut:

1 square, 2½" × 2½"

4 strips, 1½" × 4½"

4 rectangles, 1½" × 2½"

24 squares, 1½" × 1½"

From the light print, cut:

2 strips, 2" × 42"; crosscut into:

    2 strips, 2" × 13½"

    2 strips, 2" × 10½"

8 strips, 1½" × 4½"

24 squares, 1½" × 1½"

2 strips, 1¼" × 42"

Making the Blocks

After sewing each seam, press the seam allowances as indicated by the arrows.

1. Lay out five blue 1½" squares and four light 1½" squares as shown. Sew the squares together to make a block. Make four Nine Patch blocks that measure 3½" square.

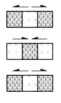

Make 4.

2. Join two light 1½" × 4½" strips and one blue 1½" × 4½" strip as shown to make a Rail Fence block that measures 3½" × 4½". Make four.

Make 4.

Pieced and hand quilted by Sue Bennett

3. Draw a diagonal line on the wrong side of the remaining light 1½" squares. Place a marked square on one end of a blue 1½" × 2½" rectangle. Stitch on the marked line. Trim ¼" from the stitching line. Flip the triangle up and press. Repeat on the opposite end of the rectangle, positioning the square as shown. Make four flying-geese units that are 1½" × 2½".

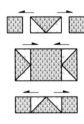

Make 4.

4. Lay out four blue 1½" squares, four flying-geese units, and one blue 2½" square as shown. Sew the pieces together into rows. Join the rows to make a Star block measuring 4½" square.

Make 1.

Assembling the Quilt Top

After sewing each seam, press the seam allowances as indicated by the arrows.

1. Lay out the Nine Patch blocks, Rail Fence blocks, and Star block in three rows as shown. Sew the blocks together. Sew the rows together. The quilt should measure 10½" square.

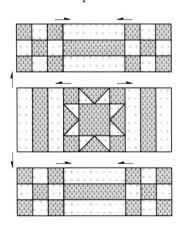

2. Sew light 2" × 10½" strips to opposite sides of the quilt. Sew light 2" × 13½" strips to the top and bottom of the quilt.

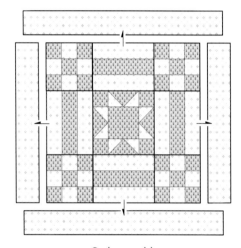

Quilt assembly

Finishing the Quilt

1. For free, downloadable help with the following steps, go to ShopMartingale.com/HowtoQuilt. Layer the quilt top, batting, and backing; baste the layers together.

2. Sue quilted an X in the Star block and lines through each patch in the Nine Patch and Rail Fence blocks. She finished by quilting double lines through the borders.

3. Attach the binding to the quilt, referring to "Single-Fold Binding" on page 78.

Hexagon Garden

FINISHED QUILT: 14½" × 14½" ✿ FINISHED BORDER BLOCK: 2" × 2"

A garden is always a lovely thing, and a scrappy quilt made from little hexagon flowers brings the garden indoors. Enjoy a little easy piecing along with some simple appliqué and you've got your very own lovely garden ready to hang on a wall.

Materials

Yardage is based on 42"-wide fabric.

¼ yard *total* of assorted light prints for blocks and hexagons

¼ yard *total* of assorted medium and dark prints for blocks and hexagons

⅛ yard of dark blue print for side borders

⅛ yard of red print for binding

1 square, 6" × 6", of 4 different light shirting prints for background

1 rectangle, 3" × 4", of red stripe for small leaves

1 square, 7" × 7", of green stripe for large leaves

1 rectangle, 3" × 5", of green print A for stems

1 square, 5" × 5", of green print B for stem

½ yard of fabric for backing

18" × 18" piece of low-loft cotton batting

Fabric glue

Several sheets of cardstock or heavyweight paper for hexagon template

Single-hole paper punch (optional)

Heat-resistant template plastic for leaf appliqués

¼" pressing bar for stems

Cutting

From *each* light shirting square, cut:
1 square, 5½" × 5½" (4 total)

From the assorted light prints, cut:
5 squares, 1⅞" × 1⅞"; cut the squares in half diagonally to yield 10 triangles
20 squares, 1½" × 1½"
3 squares, 2" × 2"

From the assorted medium and dark prints, cut:
3 sets of 6 matching 2" × 2" squares (18 total)
11 squares, 1⅞" × 1⅞"; cut the squares in half diagonally to yield 22 triangles
20 squares, 1½" × 1½"
19 squares, 2" × 2"

From green print A, cut *on the bias*:
2 strips, 1¼" × 4"

From green print B, cut *on the bias*:
1 strip, 1¼" × 6½"

From the dark blue print, cut:
2 strips, 2½" × 10½"

From the red print, cut:
2 strips, 1¼" × 42"

Pieced and hand quilted by Kathleen Tracy

Making the Appliqué Background

Sew the light 5½" squares together to make a four-patch unit measuring 10½" square. Press the seam allowances as indicated by the arrows.

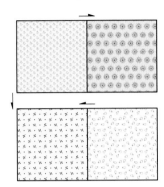

Preparing the Hexagon Templates

You will need seven hexagon templates for each flower. To make the templates, you have several options.

Make your own. Use the pattern below to make a template. Then trace the template onto cardstock or heavy paper and cut out the shape carefully on the lines.

Print hexagons from the Internet. I used a website that allows you to print hexagons of any size. Print a grid of hexagons with sides equal to 0.6". That's the size I used to create 3" flowers. Print directly onto cardstock; cut the hexagons apart one at a time. (The website is incompetech.com/graphpaper/hexagonal/.)

Purchase precut paper hexagons. There are several companies that make paper hexagon shapes you can purchase in different sizes to use as templates. You can find them at quilt shops, online, or at quilt shows. Choose hexagon templates that measure ⅝" along the sides or 1" from flat side to flat side.

Hexagon
Make 21.

PUNCH A HOLE

After cutting out the shapes, place a dot in the center of each paper hexagon and use a hole punch to make a single hole. The hole makes it easy to pin the templates to the fabric. It also makes it easy to remove the paper templates with the edge of a seam ripper after the pieces have been stitched together.

Making the Hexagon Flowers

For each hexagon flower, choose six matching 2" squares for the petals and one contrasting square for the center.

1. Place a paper hexagon in the center of the wrong side of a 2" square. Secure the paper to the fabric by placing a small pin through the hole. Cut around the shape, leaving a generous ¼" all around.

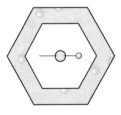

2. Fold over one edge and then fold over the next edge. Baste the corner. Go around the hexagon, stitching down all the sides and being careful not to catch the paper. Finish with a knot to secure. Repeat for the six matching hexagons and the contrasting center hexagon. Remove the pin and leave the paper pieces inside.

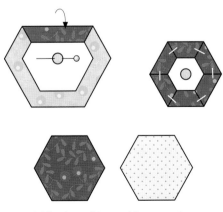

Make 6 matching and 1 contrasting hexagon for each flower.

3. Place the center hexagon right sides together with another hexagon. Whipstitch the sides together, catching just the edges of the fabric.

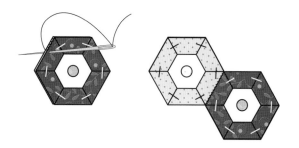

4. Continue adding the remaining hexagons around the edges of the center hexagon in a circular fashion.

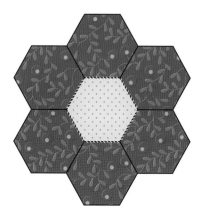

5. Connect the sides of the outer hexagons by placing them right sides together, folding the paper if necessary. When you've finished a flower, use the tip of a seam ripper to gently remove the paper hexagons. Press them flat. Make three flowers.

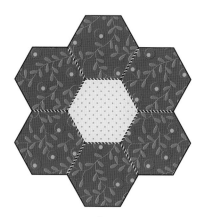

Make 3.

Making the Stems and Leaves

1. Using the patterns on page 29, trace the small leaf and large leaf onto template plastic and cut out on the line. Referring to "Appliqué" on page 77, use the red-stripe rectangle to make two small leaves. Use the green-stripe rectangle to make two large leaves.

2. Referring to "Making Bias Stems" on page 78, use the green 1¼" × 6½" bias strip to make one stem. Use the green 1¼" × 4" bias strips to make two stems.

Making the Pieced Border

After sewing each seam, press the seam allowances as indicated by the arrows.

1. Randomly select four light, medium, or dark 1½" squares. Sew the squares together to make a Four Patch block as shown. Make six Four Patch blocks measuring 2½" square.

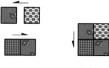

Make 6.

2. Sew the 1⅞" triangles together in pairs to make 16 half-square-triangle units measuring 1½" square.

Make 16.

3. Lay out two light, medium, or dark 1½" squares and two half-square-triangle units as shown. Sew the pieces together as shown. Make eight Homeward Bound blocks measuring 2½" square.

Make 8.

Assembling the Quilt Top

1. Place the 6½"-long stem along the center seam on the four-patch background unit, glue baste, and pin in place. Place the 4"-long stems on opposite sides of the center stem as shown in the appliqué placement guide, tucking them under the center stem. Glue baste and pin in place. Appliqué the stems.

2. Position the leaves as shown; glue baste and pin in place. Appliqué the leaves to the background. Place a small dot of fabric glue on the back of each hexagon flower. Place the center of the flowers at the ends of the stems and appliqué in place.

Appliqué placement guide

3. Sew dark blue strips to opposite sides of the quilt. Press the seam allowances toward the borders.

4. Join three Four Patch blocks and four Homeward Bound blocks to make a top border row measuring 2½" × 14½". Press the seam allowances toward the Four Patch blocks. Repeat to make a bottom border row. Sew the rows to the top and bottom

of the quilt as shown below. Press the seam allowances toward the center.

Quilt assembly

Finishing the Quilt

1. For free, downloadable help with the following steps, go to ShopMartingale.com/HowtoQuilt. Layer the quilt top, batting, and backing; baste the layers together.

2. Quilt in the ditch around the appliquéd portion of the quilt. Quilt around the shapes. Stitch a line through the center of the leaves and through each hexagon flower petal. Quilt two vertical lines ½" apart in the side borders of the quilt. Quilt an X in each block along the top and bottom borders.

3. Attach the binding to the quilt, referring to "Single-Fold Binding" on page 78.

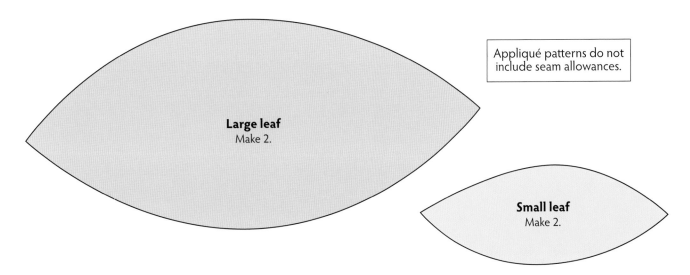

Large leaf
Make 2.

Appliqué patterns do not include seam allowances.

Small leaf
Make 2.

Honeybee

FINISHED QUILT: 15" × 15"

Working with several different prints of the same color is a good way to lend a scrappy feel to a simple quilt. Quilters from the past utilized this technique when fabric was scarce or they ran out of a certain fabric and had to "make do" with another. Inspired by an antique doll quilt, this simple quilt in many shades of brown is perfect if you're a beginner at appliqué, and it makes a charming wall hanging or topper for a small table.

Materials

Yardage is based on 42"-wide fabric.

⅛ yard of light print for inner border

⅛ yard of medium brown print for outer border

1 square, 6" × 6", of tan print for center square

1 square, 7" × 7", of red print for corner blocks

12 squares, 3" × 3", of assorted brown prints for appliqués

⅛ yard of dark brown print for binding

⅝ yard of fabric for backing

19" × 19" piece of low-loft cotton batting

Heat-resistant template plastic for appliqués

Cutting

From the light print, cut:
2 strips, 2½" × 10"
2 strips, 2½" × 6"

From the medium brown print, cut:
4 strips, 3" × 10"

From the red print, cut:
4 squares, 3" × 3"

From the dark brown print, cut:
2 strips, 1¼" × 42"

Making the Quilt Top

After sewing each seam, press the seam allowances as indicated by the arrows.

1. Sew light 2½" × 6" strips to opposite sides of the tan 6" square. Sew light 2½" × 10" strips to the top and bottom of the square. The quilt center should measure 10" square.

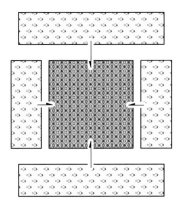

Pieced and hand quilted by Kathleen Tracy

2. Sew medium brown strips to opposite sides of the quilt center. Sew a red square to each end of a remaining medium brown strip. Make two and sew them to the top and bottom of the quilt.

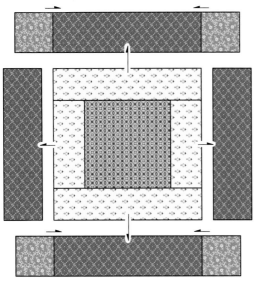

Quilt assembly

Appliquéing the Petals

1. Using the pattern below, trace the appliqué shape onto template plastic and cut out on the line. Referring to "Appliqué" on page 77, use the brown 3" squares to make 12 petals.

2. Position three petals in each corner of the light border as shown in the photo on page 32. Appliqué the shapes in place.

Finishing the Quilt

1. For free, downloadable help with the following steps, go to ShopMartingale.com/HowtoQuilt. Layer the quilt top, batting, and backing; baste the layers together.

2. Quilt in the ditch around the center block. Quilt around the petals. Quilt two parallel lines ½" apart in the borders and an X in the corner blocks.

3. Attach the binding to the quilt, referring to "Single-Fold Binding" on page 78.

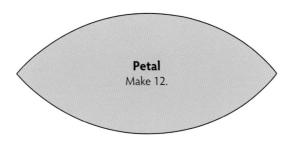

Petal
Make 12.

Appliqué patterns do not include seam allowances.

Crow's Foot

FINISHED QUILT: 15½" × 15½" ❧ FINISHED BLOCK: 12" × 12"

Have you ever thought about the names used for old quilt blocks? Some are wonderful and evoke memories of the past. Here's another creative quilt-block pattern that was inspired by something quilters viewed in their everyday surroundings.

Materials

Yardage is based on 42"-wide fabric.

¼ yard of cream print for block
¼ yard of red-and-brown print for border
⅛ yard of dark red print for block
1 square, 10" × 10", of coral print for block
⅛ yard of brown print for binding
⅝ yard of fabric for backing
19" × 19" piece of low-loft cotton batting

Cutting

From the cream print, cut:
2 squares, 4½" × 4½"
8 squares, 2⅞" × 2⅞"
2 squares, 2½" × 2½"

From the dark red print, cut:
8 squares, 2⅞" × 2⅞"
2 squares, 2½" × 2½"

From the coral print, cut:
2 squares, 4½" × 4½"

From the red-and-brown print, cut:
2 strips, 2" × 15½"
2 strips, 2" × 12½"

From the brown print, cut:
2 strips, 1¼" × 42"

Making the Block

After sewing each seam, press the seam allowances as indicated by the arrows.

1. Draw a diagonal line from corner to corner on the wrong side of each cream 2⅞" square. Layer a marked square on top of a dark red 2⅞" square, right sides together. Stitch ¼" from both sides of the line. Cut the squares apart on the drawn line to make two half-square-triangle units. Trim the dog-ear pieces at the corners. Make 16 units that are 2½" square.

Make 16.

Pieced and hand quilted by Kathleen Tracy

2. Sew the half-square-triangle units together in pairs as shown. Make four units with the red triangles on the left and four with the red triangles on the right (eight total). The units should measure 2½" × 4½".

Make 4 of each.

3. Lay out one of each unit from step 2, one coral square, and one dark red 2½" square as shown. Sew the pieces together into rows. Join the rows and press. Make two units measuring 6½" square.

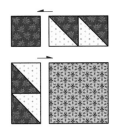 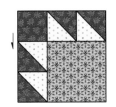

Make 2.

4. Lay out one of each unit from step 2, one cream 4½" square, and one cream 2½" square as shown. Sew the pieces together into rows. Join the rows and press. Make two units measuring 6½" square.

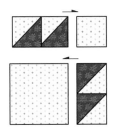 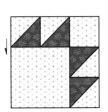

Make 2.

5. Lay out the units from steps 3 and 4 in two rows, alternating the light and dark units as shown. Sew the units together into rows. Join the rows and press. The block should measure 12½" square.

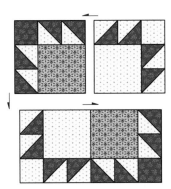

Assembling the Quilt Top

Sew red-and-brown 2" × 12½" strips to opposite sides of the quilt. Sew red-and-brown 2" × 15½" strips to the top and bottom of the quilt. Press all seam allowances toward the border.

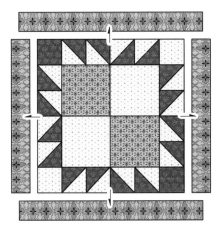

Quilt assembly

Finishing the Quilt

1. For free, downloadable help with the following steps, go to ShopMartingale.com/HowtoQuilt. Layer the quilt top, batting, and backing; baste the layers together.

2. Quilt in the ditch around each block and around the border; outline the triangles. Quilt diagonal lines in the red and coral squares. Quilt a small floral design in the center of each light square.

3. Attach the binding to the quilt, referring to "Single-Fold Binding" on page 78.

Windowpane

FINISHED QUILT: 17" × 17" ❧ **FINISHED BLOCK: 3½" × 3½"**

This little quilt was inspired by some simple blocks in an antique quilt. While the color combinations were dull, the way the quilter mismatched squares in a few of her patches intrigued me. Did she run out, or was this a way of injecting a bit of interest in a rather plain quilt? To echo her approach, I used blue prints along with a few bright pink squares to perk things up and provide a nice vintage look.

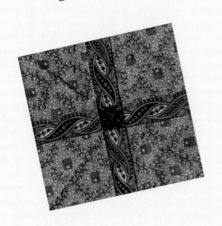

Materials

Yardage is based on 42"-wide fabric.

⅓ yard *total* of assorted light, medium, and dark prints for blocks
¼ yard of blue print for outer border
⅛ yard of brown print for inner border
⅛ yard of red print for binding
⅝ yard of fabric for backing
20" × 20" piece of low-loft cotton batting

Cutting

From the assorted light, medium, and dark prints, cut:
32 squares, 2" × 2" (8 sets of 4 matching squares)
4 squares, 2" × 2" (2 sets of 2 matching squares)
36 rectangles, 1" × 2" (9 sets of 4 matching rectangles)
9 squares, 1" × 1" (assorted)

From the brown print, cut:
2 strips, 1½" × 13"
2 strips, 1½" × 11"

From the blue print, cut:
2 strips, 2½" × 17"
2 strips, 2½" × 13"

From the red print, cut:
2 strips, 1¼" × 42"

Making the Blocks

After sewing each seam, press the seam allowances as indicated by the arrows.

For each block, choose four matching 2" squares from one light, medium, or dark print and four matching 1" × 2" rectangles from a different print. The rectangles should contrast with the squares. Choose a 1" square from a third fabric.

Lay out the squares and rectangles in three rows as shown. Sew the pieces together in rows. Join the rows and press. Make nine blocks that measure 4" square.

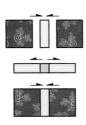

Make 9.

Pieced and hand quilted by Kathleen Tracy

2. Sew brown 1½" × 11" strips to opposite sides of the quilt. Sew brown 1½" × 13" strips to the top and bottom of the quilt.

3. Sew blue 2½" × 13" strips to opposite sides of the quilt. Sew blue 2½" × 17" strips to the top and bottom of the quilt.

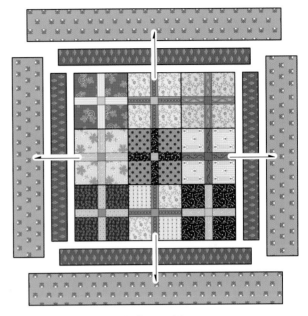

Quilt assembly

Assembling the Quilt Top

After sewing each seam, press the seam allowances as indicated by the arrows.

1. Lay out the blocks in three rows of three blocks each, rearranging the blocks until you find a pleasing arrangement. Sew the blocks together into rows. Join the rows and press. The quilt center should measure 11" square.

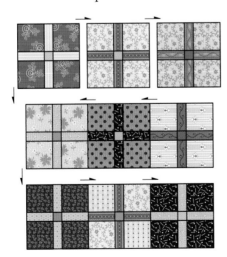

Finishing the Quilt

1. For free, downloadable help with the following steps, go to ShopMartingale.com/HowtoQuilt. Layer the quilt top, batting, and backing; baste the layers together.

2. Quilt an X in each block and in the ditch around the center of the quilt. Quilt diagonal lines 1" apart in the outer border.

3. Attach the binding to the quilt, referring to "Single-Fold Binding" on page 78.

Disappearing Four-Patch Runner

FINISHED QUILT: 6⅛" × 17½" ⚓ FINISHED BLOCK: 4" × 4"

Little runners like this are quick and easy to make if you're short on time but still feel the need to make something to inspire your creativity. It's fun to place them on small tables or shelves around the home. Or, you can hang them vertically on a wall among your other small quilts.

Materials

Yardage is based on 42"-wide fabric.

¼ yard of light or shirting print for setting triangles

⅛ yard of blue print for blocks

⅛ yard *total* of 2 different tan prints for blocks

⅛ yard of red-and-white check for binding

¼ yard of fabric for backing

9" × 21" piece of low-loft cotton batting

Cutting

From the blue print, cut:

6 squares, 3" × 3"

From the tan prints, cut a *total* of:

6 squares, 3" × 3"

From the light or shirting print, cut:

1 square, 7" × 7"; cut the square into quarters diagonally to yield 4 setting triangles

2 squares, 3¾" × 3¾"; cut the squares in half diagonally to yield 4 corner triangles

From the red-and-white check, cut:

2 strips, 1¼" × 42"

Making the Blocks

After sewing each seam, press the seam allowances as indicated by the arrows.

1. Sew two blue squares and two tan squares together to make a four-patch unit as shown. Make three units that measure 5½" square.

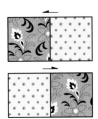
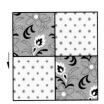

Make 3.

Pieced and hand quilted by Kathleen Tracy

2. Place a block on a small cutting mat so it's easy to turn. Measure ¾" from the center seam and use a rotary cutter to make the first cut. Without moving the pieces, rotate the block 90°. Measure ¾" from the center seam and make a second cut. Rotate the block 90°, measure ¾" from the center seam, and make a third cut. Rotate the block 90° again, measure ¾" from the center seam, and make the last cut. You should have nine sections as shown.

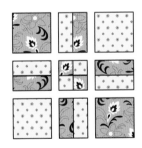

3. Rotate each rectangular section 180° as shown. Sew the pieces together into rows and then join the rows to make a block. For a scrappy look, switch the rectangular sections in one block with the rectangular sections from another block as shown in the middle and bottom blocks in the photo on page 44. Make three blocks that measure 4½" square. (The block is sometimes called a Counterchange Cross block.)

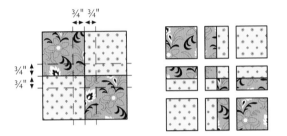

Make 3.

Assembling the Runner

Sew the blocks and light 7" setting triangles together in diagonal rows as shown. Press the seam allowances toward the setting triangles. Add the light 3¾" triangles to the corners. Trim and square up the table runner, making sure to leave ¼" beyond the points of all the blocks for seam allowances.

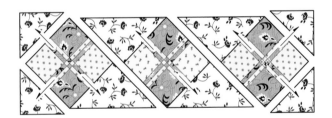

Runner assembly

Finishing the Runner

1. For free, downloadable help with the following steps, go to ShopMartingale.com/HowtoQuilt. Layer the quilt top, batting, and backing; baste the layers together.

2. Quilt an X in the blocks and a 1" crosshatch design in the setting pieces.

3. Attach the binding to the quilt, referring to "Single-Fold Binding" on page 78.

Pink-and-Brown Nine Patch

FINISHED QUILT: 17" × 17" ⚘ **FINISHED BLOCK: 3" × 3"**

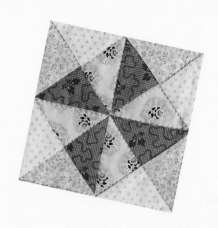

I love to play around with Nine Patch blocks because they're quick to stitch. Even a beginner can make them in no time at all. One of my favorite color combinations is pink and brown, and along with the muted light prints, the pinks and browns give this quilt a timeworn look.

Materials

Yardage is based on 42"-wide fabric.
¼ yard *total* of assorted pink prints for blocks
¼ yard *total* of assorted light prints for blocks
⅛ yard *total* of assorted brown prints for blocks
⅛ yard of dark brown print for border
⅛ yard of light pink print for border
⅛ yard of pink print for binding
⅝ yard of fabric for backing
20" × 20" piece of low-loft cotton batting

Cutting

From the assorted pink prints, cut:
44 squares, 1½" × 1½" (11 sets of 4 matching squares)
4 assorted squares, 1½" × 1½"
1 square, 4¼" × 4¼"; cut the squares into quarters diagonally to yield 4 triangles

From the assorted brown prints, cut:
12 squares, 1½" × 1½" (3 sets of 4 matching squares)
4 assorted squares, 1½" × 1½"

From the assorted light prints, cut:
40 squares, 1½" × 1½" (10 sets of 4 matching squares)
4 assorted squares, 1½" × 1½"
3 assorted squares, 4¼" × 4¼"; cut the squares into quarters diagonally to yield 12 triangles

From the light pink print, cut:
2 strips, 2¾" × 12½"

From the dark brown print, cut:
2 strips, 2¾" × 17"

From the pink print, cut:
2 strips, 1¼" × 42"

Pieced and hand quilted by Kathleen Tracy

Making the Nine Patch Blocks

After sewing each seam, press the seam allowances as indicated by the arrows.

Choose four matching pink (or brown) 1½" squares and four matching light (or pink) 1½" squares. Choose a contrasting light, pink, or brown square for the center of the block. Lay out the squares in three rows of three squares each as shown. Join the squares into rows. Join the rows and press. Make 12 blocks that measure 3½" square.

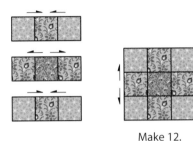

Make 12.

Making the Hourglass Blocks

After sewing each seam, press the seam allowances as indicated by the arrows.

1. Choose three different light triangles and one pink triangle. Sew two light triangles together along their short sides as shown. Sew one light triangle and one pink triangle together in the same manner as shown. Make four of each unit.

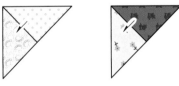

Make 4 of each.

2. Join one of each unit as shown to make an Hourglass block. Make four blocks that measure 3½" square.

Make 4.

Assembling the Quilt Top

After sewing each seam, press the seam allowances as indicated by the arrows.

1. Sew four Nine Patch blocks together to make a row. Make two rows that measure 3½" × 12½".

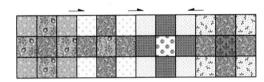

Make 2.

2. Sew two Nine Patch blocks together to make a vertical row. Make two rows that measure 3½" × 6½".

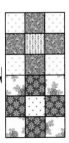

Make 2.

3. Sew the Hourglass blocks together, rotating them as shown to make a pink pinwheel in the center. The block should measure 6½" square.

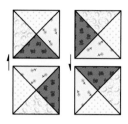
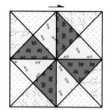

Make 1.

4. Sew the Nine Patch rows from step 2 to opposite sides of the block from step 3. Sew the Nine Patch rows from step 1 to the top and bottom of the quilt. Press. The quilt center should measure 12½" square.

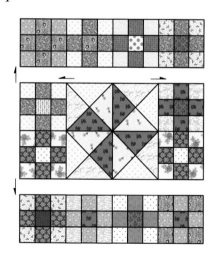

5. Sew light pink 2¾" × 12½" border strips to opposite sides of the quilt. Sew dark brown 2¾" × 17" border strips to the top and bottom of the quilt. Press.

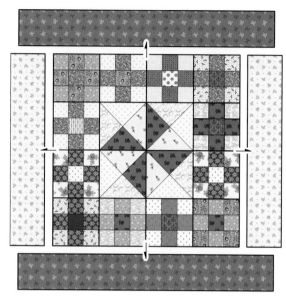

Quilt assembly

Finishing the Quilt

1. For free, downloadable help with the following steps, go to ShopMartingale.com/HowtoQuilt. Layer the quilt top, batting, and backing; baste the layers together.

2. Quilt an X in each Nine Patch block and outline quilt the Hourglass blocks in the center. Mark and then quilt parallel wavy lines in the borders.

3. Attach the binding to the quilt, referring to "Single-Fold Binding" on page 78.

Indigo-and-Pink Sixteen Patch

FINISHED QUILT: 17¾" × 17¾" ⚜ FINISHED BLOCK: 6" × 6"

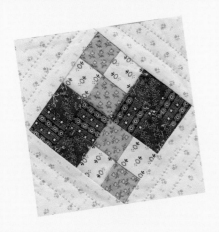

Before the invention of the sewing machine in the mid-nineteenth century, women had to make all the family clothing, bedding, and linens by hand. It made sense that the earlier a girl learned how to sew, the sooner she could help out with family sewing chores. There were so many! Some mothers knew that teaching daughters to make clothing and quilts for their dolls was a good way to infuse a bit of play into the lessons and motivate children to perfect their sewing skills. With a little help, a simple quilt like this—with Four Patches sewn together and set on point—may have been just right for a beginner.

Materials

Yardage is based on 42"-wide fabric.
¼ yard *total* of 8 different light prints for blocks
¼ yard *total* of assorted pink prints for blocks
¼ yard of indigo print for border
⅛ yard of brown print for sashing (brown A)
1 square, 4" × 4", *each* of 2 different medium blue prints for blocks
1 square, 4" × 4", *each* of 2 different dark blue prints for blocks
1 square, 4" × 4", *each* of 2 different gray prints for blocks
1 rectangle, 4" × 7", of blue check for blocks
⅛ yard of brown fabric for binding (brown B)
⅝ yard of backing fabric
21" × 21" piece of low-loft cotton batting

Cutting

From the assorted pink prints, cut:
16 squares, 1½" × 1½" (4 sets of 4 matching squares)
8 squares, 1½" × 1½" (4 sets of 2 matching squares)
1 square, 1¾" × 1¾"

From *each* of 4 assorted light prints, cut:
6 squares, 1½" × 1½" (24 total)

From *each* of the remaining 4 assorted light prints, cut:
2 squares, 3⅞" × 3⅞" (8 total); cut the squares in half diagonally to yield 16 triangles

From *each* of the medium blue prints, cut:
4 squares, 1½" × 1½" (8 total)

From *each* of the dark blue prints, cut:
4 squares, 1½" × 1½" (8 total)

From *each* of the gray prints, cut:
4 squares, 1½" × 1½" (8 total)

From the blue check, cut:
8 squares, 1½" × 1½"

From brown A, cut:
4 strips, 1¾" × 6½"

From the indigo print, cut:
4 strips, 2½" × 13¾"

From brown B, cut:
2 strips, 1¼" × 42"

Pieced and hand quilted by Kathleen Tracy

Making the Blocks

After sewing each seam, press the seam allowances as indicated by the arrows.

1. Lay out two matching pink 1½" squares and two matching light 1½" squares in two rows as shown. Sew the squares together to make a pink four-patch unit. Make 12 units that measure 2½" square. Set aside four units for the border.

Make 12.

2. Lay out two matching medium blue squares and two matching gray squares in two rows as shown. Sew the squares together to make a blue four-patch unit. Make four units that measure 2½" square. In the same way, make four units using the matching dark blue squares and the blue check squares for a total of eight blue units.

Make 8.

3. Lay out two matching units from step 1 and two matching units from step 2 as shown. Join the units into rows. Join the rows and press. Make four blocks that measure 4½" square.

Make 4.

4. Sew matching light triangles to opposite sides of each block from step 3. Sew matching triangles to the remaining sides of the blocks. Square up the blocks to measure 6½" square.

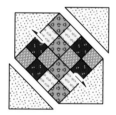 

Make 4.

Assembling the Quilt Top

After sewing each seam, press the seam allowances as indicated by the arrows.

1. Sew two blocks and one 1¾" × 6½" brown A strip together to make a block row. Make two block rows that measure 6½" × 13¾".

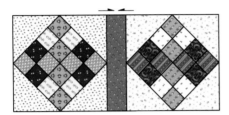

Make 2.

2. Sew two 1¾" × 6½" brown A strips and the pink 1¾" square together to make a sashing row that measures 1¾" × 13¾".

Make 1.

3. Sew the block rows and sashing row together as shown to make the quilt center. The quilt center should measure 13¾" square.

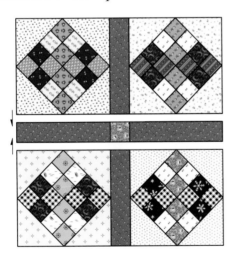

4. Sew indigo 2½" × 13¾" strips to opposite sides of the quilt. Sew a pink four-patch unit from step 1 of "Making the Blocks" to each end of an indigo 2½" × 13¾" strip, arranging the pink squares so they point outward as shown. Make two and sew them to the top and bottom of the quilt.

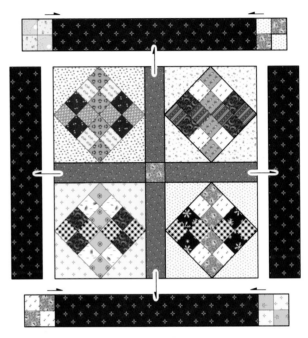

Quilt assembly

Finishing the Quilt

1. For free, downloadable help with the following steps, go to ShopMartingale.com/HowtoQuilt. Layer the quilt top, batting, and backing; baste the layers together.

2. Quilt an X design in each block and in the ditch around the center of the quilt. Quilt diagonal lines in the light print setting triangles. Quilt parallel lines in the sashing and an X in the center. Quilt diamonds and an X in the corner blocks.

3. Attach the binding to the quilt, referring to "Single-Fold Binding" on page 78.

Square in a Square

FINISHED QUILT: 17½" × 22" ❧ FINISHED BLOCK: 3½" × 3½"

A unique block in a quilt top from the late 1800s inspired this little quilt. I was struck by the contrast among the many different dark prints, and I loved how the quilter used her fabrics to create an almost contemporary look with the simple square-in-a-square design. I tried to imitate her style, keeping to the darker fabrics. I mixed in a few blue prints and added a taupe sashing for a soft contrast.

Materials

Yardage is based on 42"-wide fabrics.

½ yard *total* of assorted light, medium, and dark prints for blocks

¼ yard of light taupe print for sashing

5" × 7" rectangle of red print for sashing squares

¼ yard of brown print for binding

¾ yard of fabric for backing

21" × 25" piece of low-loft cotton batting

Cutting

From the assorted light, medium, and dark prints, cut:

20 squares, 3" × 3"

40 squares, 2⅝" × 2⅝"; cut the squares in half diagonally to yield 80 triangles

From the light taupe print, cut:

4 strips, 1½" × 42"; crosscut into 31 pieces, 1½" × 4"

From the red print, cut:

12 squares, 1½" × 1½"

From the brown print, cut:

3 strips, 1¼" × 42"

Making the Blocks

After sewing each seam, press the seam allowances as indicated by the arrows.

For each block, choose a light, medium, or dark square and four contrasting triangles—two from one print and two from a different print.

1. Sew matching triangles to opposite sides of the square as shown.

2. Sew matching triangles to the remaining two sides of the square as shown. Make 20 blocks. Trim the blocks to measure 4" square.

Make 20.

Pieced and machine quilted by Kathleen Tracy

Assembling the Quilt Top

After sewing each seam, press the seam allowances as indicated by the arrows.

1. Sew four blocks and three taupe sashing strips together to make a row. Make five rows that measure 4" × 17½".

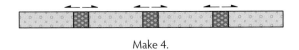

Make 5.

2. Sew four taupe sashing strips and three red squares together to make a sashing row. Make four sashing rows that measure 1½" × 17½".

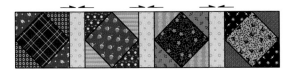

Make 4.

3. Sew the block rows and sashing rows together as shown.

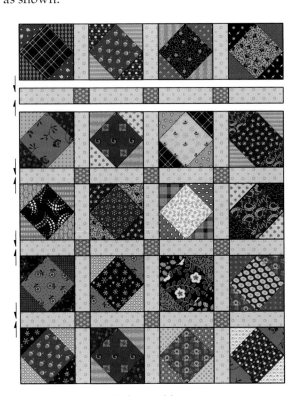

Quilt assembly

Finishing the Quilt

1. For free, downloadable help with the following steps, go to ShopMartingale.com/HowtoQuilt. Layer the quilt top, batting, and backing; baste the layers together.

2. Quilt a line through the middle of each sashing strip. Quilt diagonal lines through the centers of the blocks and sashing squares.

3. Attach the binding to the quilt, referring to "Single-Fold Binding" on page 78.

Papa's Shirts

FINISHED QUILT: 12½" × 12½"   ❧   FINISHED BLOCK: 3" × 3"

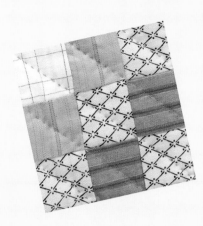

When I began working on this book, my original title was Papa's Shirts and Mama's Dresses to reflect the notion that many antique scrap quilts contained scraps of old clothing. My friend Sue didn't know this when she gifted me with a small quilt last Christmas as I was working on this book. Imagine my delight when I opened the package and found out that my new little quilt was inspired by a photo of an antique doll quilt I had sent to her. Not only that, Sue had made the quilt using scraps from cast-off shirts belonging to her husband Charlie! How fitting to include this quilt in this collection.

Materials

Yardage is based on 42"-wide fabric.

¼ yard of a dark blue print for border

1 fat quarter (18" × 21") of gray stripe for blocks and binding

⅛ yard *total* of assorted light, tan, or shirting prints for blocks

⅛ yard *total* of assorted medium or dark blue prints for blocks

4" x 5" rectangle of red stripe for blocks

½ yard of fabric for backing

16" × 16" piece of low-loft cotton batting

Cutting

From the assorted light, tan, or shirting prints, cut:
38 squares, 1½" × 1½"

From the assorted medium or dark blue prints, cut:
32 squares, 1½" × 1½"

From the red stripe, cut:
5 squares, 1½" × 1½"

From the gray stripe, cut:
6 squares, 1½" × 1½"
60" of 1¼"-wide bias binding

From the dark blue print, cut:
2 strips, 2" × 12½"
2 strips, 2" × 9½"

Making the Nine Patch Blocks

1. Arrange four matching light squares and five matching dark squares (blue, red, or gray) as shown. Sew the squares together into rows. Press the seam allowances toward the dark squares. Join the rows, matching the seam intersections. Press the seam allowances toward the center. Make three blocks that measure 3½" square.

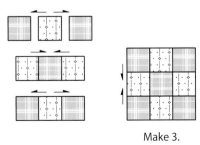

Make 3.

Pieced and hand quilted by Sue Bennett

2. Repeat step 1, using four matching dark squares and five matching light squares to make two blocks that measure 3½" square.

Make 2.

3. Make one block using two sets of two matching dark squares, one set of four matching light squares, and one mismatched light square. Using the remaining 13 light squares and 14 dark squares, make three blocks with one mismatched square per block as shown.

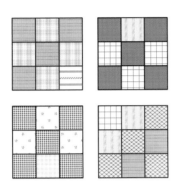

Make 1 of each.

Assembling the Quilt Top

After sewing each seam, press the seam allowances as indicated by the arrows.

1. Arrange the blocks in three rows of three blocks each as shown. Sew the blocks together into rows. Join the rows and press. The quilt center should measure 9½" square.

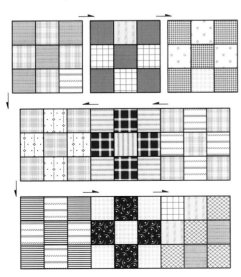

2. Sew dark blue 2" × 9½" strips to opposite sides of the quilt. Sew dark blue 2" × 12½" strips to the top and bottom of the quilt.

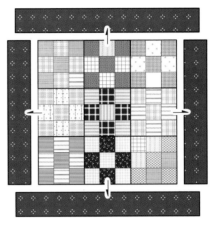

Quilt assembly

Finishing the Quilt

1. For free, downloadable help with the following steps, go to ShopMartingale.com/HowtoQuilt. Layer the quilt top, batting, and backing; baste the layers together.

2. Using light brown quilting thread, Sue hand quilted a diagonal line through the middle of each square and a line through the center of the borders for a simple finish and an old-fashioned look.

3. Attach the binding to the quilt, referring to "Single-Fold Binding" on page 78.

HAND PIECING

If you've never taken the time to hand piece a small quilt, you're in for a surprise when you find out how relaxing it can be. This quilt is one that's simple enough to hand piece and perfect for teaching to a child.

Treasure Boxes

FINISHED QUILT: 11" × 11" ⚭ FINISHED BLOCK: 3½" × 3½"

One of the most familiar and beloved of quilt patterns from the nineteenth century has to be the Log Cabin. A variation of the Log Cabin is known as Courthouse Steps, also made with strips resembling the logs in a cabin, and still popular today as part of the American quilting tradition. The finished "logs" in this vintage-looking quilt measure just ½" wide.

"I began to sew for my dolls when I was six. Mama showed me how to cut a pattern, set in sleeves, how to gather a skirt to put in a belt, how to make buttonholes, how to do hemstitching. The box of scraps from her dressmaking was my treasure box."

~Lois Lenski
Author of Strawberry Girl and other children's and young adult fiction

Materials

Yardage is based on 42"-wide fabric.

⅓ yard *total* of assorted light, medium, and dark prints for blocks

⅛ yard of dark gray solid for binding

½ yard of fabric for backing

15" × 15" piece of low-loft cotton batting

Cutting

From the assorted light, medium, and dark prints, cut:

36 strips, 1" × 2" (18 sets of 2 matching strips)

36 strips, 1" × 3" (18 sets of 2 matching strips)

18 strips, 1" × 4" (9 sets of 2 matching strips)

18 squares, 1" × 1" (9 sets of 2 matching squares)

9 contrasting squares, 1" × 1"

From the dark gray solid, cut:

2 strips, 1¼" × 42"

Making the Courthouse Steps Block

After sewing each seam, press the seam allowances away from the center square.

1. Choose two matching 1" squares and one contrasting 1" square. Sew the squares together as shown to make a 1" × 2" center unit. Make nine.

Make 9.

2. Sew matching 1" × 2" strips to the top and bottom of a unit from step 1 as shown. Make nine.

Make 9.

Pieced and hand quilted by Kathleen Tracy

3. Sew matching 1" × 2" strips to opposite sides of a unit from step 2 as shown. Sew matching 1" × 3" strips to the top and bottom of the unit. Make nine.

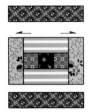

Make 9.

4. Sew matching 1" × 3" strips to opposite sides of a unit from step 3 as shown. Sew matching 1" × 4" strips to the top and bottom of the unit to complete the block. The block should measure 4" × 4". Make nine.

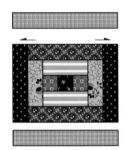

Make 9.

Treasure Box Runners

As you stitch your quilt, make a few extra blocks and create delightful little (4" x 11") runners to place around the home or give to friends.

Pieced and hand quilted by Karen Schultz

Assembling the Quilt Top

After sewing each seam, press the seam allowances as indicated by the arrows.

1. Arrange the blocks in three rows of three blocks each as shown. Sew the blocks together into rows.

2. Join the rows.

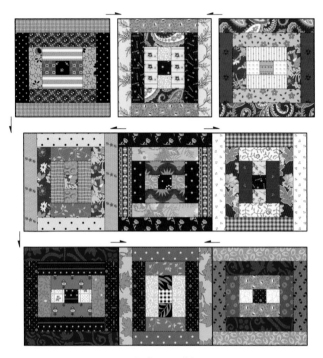

Quilt assembly

Finishing the Quilt

1. For free, downloadable help with the following steps, go to ShopMartingale.com/HowtoQuilt. Layer the quilt top, batting, and backing; baste the layers together.

2. Hand quilt a line of stitching through the lengthwise center of each strip in each block.

3. Attach the binding to the quilt, referring to "Single-Fold Binding" on page 78.

Scrap-Box Strip

FINISHED QUILT: 26¾" × 36¼" ❧ FINISHED BLOCK: 3" × 3"

I feel most creative when I can play with my fabric scraps and come up with a pleasing design using a simple block, one like the Nine Patch that's been around for hundreds of years. I used more than 55 different nineteenth-century reproduction prints to give this quilt its wonderfully scrappy look.

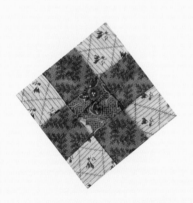

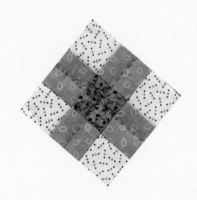

Materials

Yardage is based on 42"-wide fabric.

⅜ yard of tan shirting print for setting and corner triangles

⅓ yard *total* of assorted medium-to-dark prints in red, brown, blue, gold, green, purple, and brown for blocks

¼ yard *total* of assorted medium-to-light prints in tan, pink, blue, cream, and green for blocks

¼ yard of gold print for sashing

¼ yard of peach print for sashing

1 yard of brown-and-blue stripe for border*

¼ yard of medium blue print for border

8" square of gold plaid for border corners

¼ yard of red print for binding

1⅓ yards of fabric for backing

31" × 41" piece of low-loft cotton batting

*If you are using an allover print, you'll only need ¼ yard.

Cutting

From the assorted medium-to-light prints, cut:
84 squares, 1½" × 1½" (21 sets of 4 matching squares)

From the assorted medium-to-dark prints, cut:
84 squares, 1½" × 1½" (21 sets of 4 matching squares)
21 contrasting squares, 1½" × 1½"

From the tan shirting print, cut:
9 squares, 5½" × 5½"; cut the squares into quarters diagonally to yield 36 setting triangles
6 squares, 3" × 3"; cut the squares in half diagonally to yield 12 corner triangles

From the gold print, cut:
4 strips, 1½" × 30¼"

From the peach print, cut:
2 strips, 2¼" × 30¼"

From the brown-and-blue stripe, cut *on the lengthwise grain*:
2 strips, 3½" × 30¼"

From the gold plaid, cut:
4 squares, 3½" × 3½"

From the medium blue print, cut:
2 strips, 3½" × 20¾"

From the red print, cut:
4 strips, 1¼" × 42"

Pieced and hand quilted by Kathleen Tracy

the blocks for the seam allowances. Make three rows that measure 4¾" × 30¼".

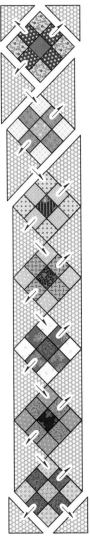

Make 3.

Making the Nine Patch Blocks

Choose four matching medium or light squares, four matching medium or dark squares, and one contrasting square. Lay out the squares in three rows as shown. Sew the squares together into rows. Press the seam allowances as indicated. Join the rows and press the seam allowances toward the center. Make 21 blocks. The blocks should measure 3½" square.

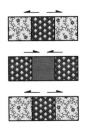

Make 21.

Assembling the Quilt Top

After sewing each seam, press the seam allowances as indicated by the arrows.

1. Lay out seven blocks, 12 large tan triangles, and four small tan corner triangles as shown. Sew the blocks and triangles together in a vertical row as shown at right. Trim and square up the row, making sure to leave ¼" beyond the points of all

CHARM QUILTS

Don't assume that every scrap quilt has to be a charm quilt with each piece cut from a different fabric. Some of my best scrappy quilts have a few favorite prints repeated here and there, and although they're not specifically charm quilts, they're still "charming."

2. Sew a gold strip to each long side of a peach strip to make a sashing unit. Make two units that measure 4¼" × 30¼".

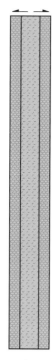

Make 2.

3. Sew the block rows from step 1 and the sashing units from step 2 together as shown to make the quilt center. The quilt center should measure 20¾" × 30¼".

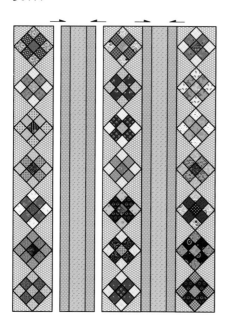

4. Sew brown-and-blue stripe strips to opposite sides of the quilt. Sew a gold plaid square to each end of a medium blue strip. Make two and sew them to the top and bottom of the quilt.

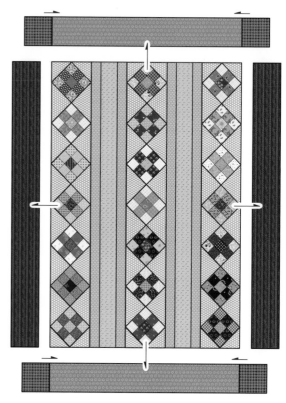

Quilt assembly

Finishing the Quilt

1. For free, downloadable help with the following steps, go to ShopMartingale.com/HowtoQuilt. Layer the quilt top, batting, and backing; baste the layers together.

2. Quilt in the ditch around the blocks and along the sashing strips. Quilt an X in the center of each block, diamonds along the peach strips, and diagonal lines and Xs in the borders and corner blocks.

3. Attach the binding to the quilt, referring to "Single-Fold Binding" on page 78.

Little Strippy

FINISHED QUILT: 12⅜" × 15⅛"   FINISHED BLOCK: 1½" × 1½"

Made with smaller blocks, this miniature version of Scrap-Box Strip is a nice companion quilt to the larger quilt on page 68. If you like working with tiny pieces, put on your magnifiers and get started. These Nine Patch blocks finish at only 1½" square!

Materials

Yardage is based on 42"-wide fabric.

¼ yard of green print for sashing strips and binding

⅛ yard *total* of assorted medium and dark prints for blocks

⅛ yard *total* of assorted light prints for blocks

⅛ yard of light blue print for setting triangles

⅛ yard of dark blue print for border

⅛ yard of rust print for border

1 square, 6" × 6", of brown print for border corners

1 fat quarter (18" × 21") of fabric for backing

16" × 19" piece of low-loft cotton batting

Cutting

From the assorted light prints, cut:
60 squares, 1" × 1" (15 sets of 4 matching squares)

From the assorted medium and dark prints, cut:
60 squares, 1" × 1" (15 sets of 4 matching squares)
15 contrasting squares, 1" × 1"

From the light blue print, cut:
6 squares, 3½" × 3½"; cut the squares into quarters diagonally to yield 24 setting triangles
6 squares, 2" × 2"; cut the squares in half diagonally to yield 12 corner triangles

From the green print, cut:
2 strips, 1¼" × 42"
2 strips, 1¼" × 11⅛"

From the dark blue print, cut:
2 strips, 2½" × 11⅛"

From the brown print, cut:
4 squares, 2½" × 2½"

From the rust print, cut:
2 strips, 2½" × 8⅜"

Pieced and hand quilted by Marian Edwards

Making the Nine Patch Blocks

After sewing each seam, press the seam allowances as indicated by the arrows.

Choose four matching light squares, four matching medium or dark squares, and one contrasting square. Lay out the squares in three rows as shown. Sew the squares together into rows. Join the rows. The blocks should measure 2" square. Make 15 blocks.

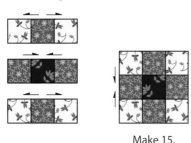

Make 15.

Assembling the Quilt Top

After sewing each seam, press the seam allowances as indicated by the arrows.

1. Lay out five blocks, eight large light blue triangles, and four small light blue corner triangles as shown. Sew together in a vertical row as shown. Trim and square up the row, leaving ¼" beyond the points of all the blocks for seam allowances. Make three rows that measure approximately 2⅝" × 11⅛".

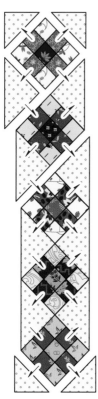

Make 3.

2. Sew the block rows from step 1 and the green 1¼" × 11⅛" strips together as shown to make the quilt center that measures 8⅜" × 11⅛".

3. Sew dark blue strips to opposite sides of the quilt. Sew a brown square to each end of a rust strip. Make two and sew them to the top and bottom of the quilt.

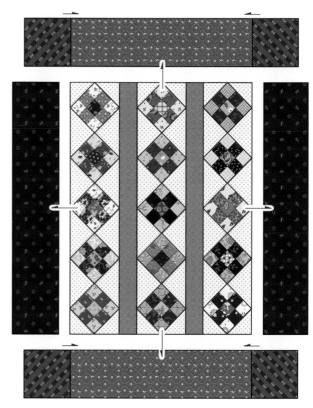

Quilt assembly

Finishing the Quilt

1. For free, downloadable help with the following steps, go to ShopMartingale.com/HowtoQuilt. Layer the quilt top, batting, and backing; baste the layers together.

2. Quilt simply, quilting an X through the blocks, double parallel lines in the sashing strips, and double parallel lines in the borders with a zigzag line between them. Outline the setting triangles and quilt a double X in the corner blocks.

3. Attach the binding to the quilt, referring to "Single-Fold Binding" on page 78.

Quiltmaking Basics

Every quilter has tried-and-true methods for making quilts, and following are some my favorites. For more, free downloadable information on a variety of quiltmaking techniques, visit Martingale's website at ShopMartingale.com/HowtoQuilt.

Appliqué

Some quilts in this book contain appliquéd pieces. My favorite method is to use starch and a heat-resistant template plastic (sometimes called No-Melt Mylar). For this method you'll need a can of spray starch, a cup, and a cotton swab or small brush.

1. Place the template plastic over the pattern and trace with a fine-line permanent marker, making sure to trace the lines exactly. Use utility scissors to cut out the template, cutting exactly on the drawn line.

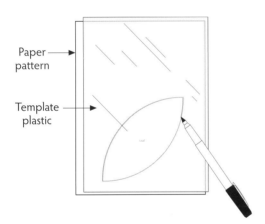

Paper pattern

Template plastic

2. Place the template on the wrong side of the chosen fabric, being careful to reverse the template if necessary for correct placement. Trace around the template using a washable fabric marker. Cut out the shape, adding a ¼"-wide seam allowance all around.

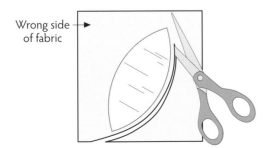

Wrong side of fabric

3. Place the appliqué shape flat, with the wrong side up, on your ironing board. Center the plastic template on the wrong side of the fabric shape. Dip the cotton swab or brush in the starch and "paint" the starch over the seam allowance of the shape.

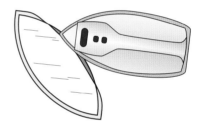

Starch

4. Using the template as a guide, and using a dry iron set on medium heat, press the seam allowance over the edge of the plastic. (The plastic will not melt but can warp if the iron is too hot.)

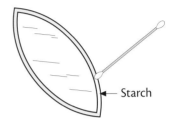

5. For outside points, fold one edge of the fabric over the template, extending the fold beyond the point of the template. Fold the other side in the same way. If you have a little fabric "flag" sticking out, do not clip the flag. Instead, to avoid fraying, fold the flag behind the point and press with your iron. There will probably be enough starch to hold the flag in place. If not, apply a slight amount of starch and press again.

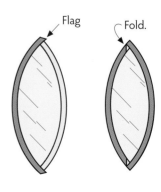

Flag

Fold.

6. Allow the piece to cool; then remove the template and re-press if needed. Position the appliqué shape on the background, using little dots of washable appliqué glue along the seam allowance, along with appliqué pins in the center, to hold the shape in place.

7. Thread a needle with a thread color that matches the appliqué fabric. Use a traditional appliqué stitch to sew the piece to the background.

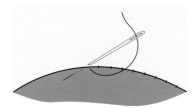

Appliqué stitch

Making Bias Stems

1. Cut the strips for stems and other pieces according to the pattern directions. Stem pieces that need to curve slightly should be cut on the bias.

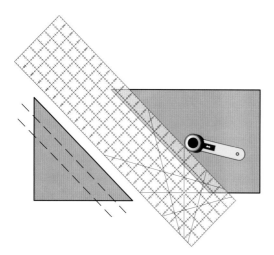

2. Fold the strips in half, wrong sides together, and press. Sew ¼" from the raw edge. Trim to ⅛".

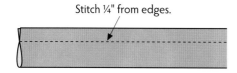

Stitch ¼" from edges.

3. Insert a pressing bar into the sewn strip or tube, turning the seam to the flat side of the bar so that it's hidden. Press the seam flat and remove the tube carefully (the pressing bars can get very hot).

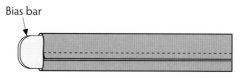

Bias bar

4. Stitch in place with an appliqué stitch according to the pattern. For appliqué stems that are curved, such as the stems in the quilt shown on page 26, gently pull the fabric to curve the stem into the shape needed.

SIMPLY QUILTED

Hand quilting a small quilt can be very relaxing. If you're a beginner and hesitant to quilt your project by hand, try quilting a simple straight line at first. Take advantage of tools that make quilting easier, like quilting stencils and water-soluble marking pens to mark your lines. There's also a special tape called Tiger Tape to help you learn to space your stitches evenly. The quilting on small quilts really doesn't have to be perfect—and you'll get better with practice. Or maybe, like me, you'll find that it won't matter if your stitches aren't perfect. They'll have that same naive charm we love so much in antique doll quilts. For more on quilting, whether by hand or by machine, see "Making a Quilt Sandwich" at ShopMartingale.com/HowtoQuilt.

Single-Fold Binding

All the quilts in this book were bound with single-fold binding, my preferred method for small quilts because it creates less bulk in the finished piece. To bind your quilt, cut 1¼"-wide strips of binding fabric, per the project instructions. Measure around the quilt and add 10" extra for mitering corners and joining strips.

1. Join the strips using a diagonal seam and press the seam allowances open.

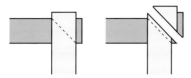

2. Using a ruler and rotary cutter, straighten the edges of the quilt and make sure the corners form right angles. Trim away the excess batting and backing.

3. Position the binding along one side of the quilt top, right sides together, and align the raw edges.

4. Leaving 5" of binding free, begin stitching the binding to the quilt top, starting at the center of one side and using a ¼" seam allowance. Sew through all three layers. Stop ¼" from the first corner and backstitch.

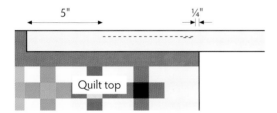

5. Remove the quilt from the machine. Turn the quilt and fold the binding straight up, making a 45° angle. Fold the binding back down, aligning it with the edge of the next side. Continue sewing the remaining sides in this way.

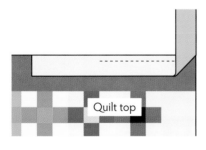

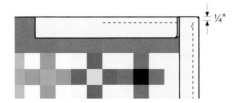

6. Stop stitching about 5" from where you started and remove the quilt from the machine. Overlap the beginning and ending pieces of binding; trim so the overlap equals the width that you cut your binding strips.

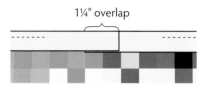

7. Place the strips right sides together at a right angle. Sew on the diagonal and trim away the excess fabric. Lay the binding back over the quilt and finish sewing it in place.

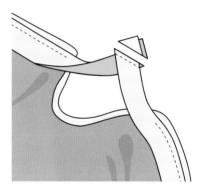

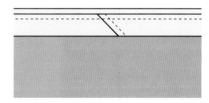

8. Fold the binding over the raw edges to the back of the quilt. Turn the raw edge under ¼" and slip-stitch it to the quilt with a blind stitch using matching thread. Miter the corners as shown.

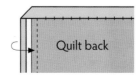

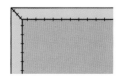

About the Author

Kathleen Tracy has been playing with fabric since childhood, when she first learned to sew. Designing quilts became a great way of expressing that early creative impulse. After working in the publishing industry for many years, she learned to quilt by making quilts for her daughter's American Girl dolls, which led to a career writing quilt-pattern books. Kathleen is best known for books that combine a little bit of history with quilts that use traditional patterns from the past. She is also the author of *The Civil War Sewing Circle* (Martingale, 2011) and *Remembering Adelia* (Martingale, 2009). When she's not quilting, she can be found reading, gardening, making jewelry, cooking, or walking and coddling her dog. Kathleen has two grown children and lives in Deerfield, Illinois, with her husband and mini-poodle pup, Ophelia. You can find Kathleen online at CountryLaneQuilts.com.

Acknowledgments

Creating a book is always a labor of love, and I could not have done it without the support of many.

Thank you to my family for their patience, support, and love—and for being so enthusiastic about all my creative endeavors.

Thank you to all the fans of my designs and books, my many online "small quilting" friends, and the steadfast followers of my blog, A Sentimental Quilter. Know that I appreciate you all very much and would not have been able to do any of this without your support and enthusiasm for small quilts these many years.

A special thanks goes to Sue Bennett, Marian Edwards, and Karen Schultz for helping out and contributing projects to this book. You're the best!

Thank you to the team at Martingale for turning my designs and ideas into a beautiful end product. Thanks to my technical editor, Nancy Mahoney, and copy editor, Durby Peterson, for making sure everything turned out perfectly. A special thanks to Karen Burns, Tina Cook, and Karen Soltys for encouraging me to "give it another go" after a long break.